DATE DUE

	JUL 17 1989
MAY 26 1980	APR 30 1991
MAY 19 1981	MAY 3 1994
	JUN 5 2000
JUL 17 1981	Jul 3 2000
	JUN 14 2001
	JUL 7 2002
APR 12 1982	
JUL 28 1982	
FEB 25 1984	
AUG 8 1985	
6/16/86	
JAN 10 1989	

How to Be
a Super
Camp Counselor

How to Be a Super Camp Counselor

BY DOREEN MANGAN
Illustrated by Terry Fehr

A Concise Guide

FRANKLIN WATTS | NEW YORK | LONDON | TORONTO | 1979

Library of Congress Cataloging in Publication Data

Mangan, Doreen.
How to be a super camp counselor.

(A Concise guide)
Bibliography: p.
Includes index.
SUMMARY: Includes advice on how to apply and
prepare for a job as camp counselor.
1. Camp counselors—Vocational guidance—Juve-
nile literature.   [1. Camp counselors—Vocational
guidance.   2. Vocational guidance]   I. Fehr, Terry.
II. Title.
GV198.C6M36   796.5′45   79–10507
ISBN 0–531–02893–3

Contents

TO MY FAMILY

ACKNOWLEDGMENTS

A number of people made important contributions to this book. I'd like to thank Andra Ellis, Ceramics Director, West Side YMCA, New York City; David Alderson, Associate Sports Fitness Director, also of the West Side YMCA; Pat Caplan, drama specialist; Pamela Galehouse, Associate Camp Director, Fresh Air Fund, New York; Dennis Buttinger, Doris Mason, Sandy Smithson of the American Camping Association, New York Division; and Dr. Ernst Bulova and Sybil Simon of the Buck's Rock Work Camp, New Milford, Connecticut.

Thanks also to Sydney Fox, Stephanie Fitzgerald, Jane Paz, and Regina Muster for ideas, and material loaned to me; and to Madeline Rogers for editing suggestions.

D.M.

How to Get a Job as a Counselor

Would you enjoy spending a summer as a camp counselor? If you've been to camp before, you may know the answer already. But if you haven't, you might like to know what is involved.

As a counselor, you'll take care of children at the camp. You'll see that they get to their activities on time, go with them on hikes and nature walks, teach them any skills you know.

You may sleep in the same cabin as they do. You'll cheer up the ones who get homesick, settle fights, sew on buttons. You probably won't earn too much money. And you'll work long hours.

But on the plus side, you'll have free room and board, a summer in the country, companionship of other counselors, and a chance to learn more about kids and develop new skills.

ARE YOU CUT OUT
TO BE A COUNSELOR?

Many young people can become good counselors, but it's not for everyone. The first requirement is that you enjoy being part of a group. As a counselor, you'll be working and living in close quarters with other counselors and staff members, as well as dozens and perhaps hundreds of kids. Which brings up an important question—do you like children? Some people, even teen-agers, feel uncomfortable around young kids. That's OK, but those people won't be happy as counselors.

Below are a few more questions to think about:

- Do you enjoy being a leader?
- Do you love the outdoor life?
- Can you start a project on your own, without being prodded into it?
- Do you finish what you start?
- Can you admit your own mistakes?
- Are you punctual?
- Can you take care of your own belongings?

If you've truthfully answered "yes" to all these questions, and if group living and working with kids appeal to you, you could be just what camp directors are looking for.

WHAT'S YOUR BACKGROUND?

There's really no one "right" kind of background needed to become a counselor. In fact, you'd be surprised at what counts in getting a camp job. The main thing is showing that you can get along well with people. One camp director says: "Being the oldest of eight children speaks for itself. You're obviously used to the give and take of living with a group of kids."

Other people-related activities include:

- Teaching a Sunday school class
- Working as a candy-striper in a hospital, especially in the pediatrics ward
- Doing volunteer work in your community center
- Spending a few hours a week working in a senior citizens' home
- Tutoring, especially in a group setting

Certain school situations provide good background for counseling, such as:

- Being on a team
- Joining a club and being an active member
- Being involved in a work-study program

Scout and 4-H experience is also valuable. And if you've been to camp before, that's a big plus.

CAN YOU TEACH A SKILL?

Almost everyone has a hobby or interest. Maybe you hike, or know how to build a fire and cook outdoors. Can you play a kazoo, guitar, or penny whistle? Can you sew, whittle, sketch, tell stories, do batik, take photographs, play volleyball? Do you know anything about birds or trees? That rock collection you've been building since you were in grade school may make you something of a geologist in the eyes of eight- or nine-year-olds.

Remember, you don't have to be an outstanding expert in what you do; just be able to do it well enough to show the kids how to do it.

HOW TO GET A JOB AT CAMP

If you decide counseling is for you, the next step is to apply for a job. The best time to do this is in winter, starting around December. That's when camp directors begin looking for counselors for the summer.

There are many different kinds of camps:

- Day camps, resident camps ("sleep-away"), travel camps
- Private-independent camps, church camps, organization camps, such as Y and Scout camps
- Specialized-clientele or specialized-program camps— for example, for the handicapped or retarded, for the performing arts, for crafts, for sports

Some camps are coed; others are for boys only or for girls only.

Jobs and responsibilities are different in each camp. And at many camps you must be at least eighteen in order to work as a counselor. But it is possible for younger people to get positions as junior counselors, counselors-in-training (CITs), program aids, waiters or waitresses. You may not earn as much as a regular counselor. In some cases, you pay a lower camper's fee. But you gain lots of good experience that can help you get a counseling job when you are older.

WHERE THE CAMPS ARE

There are thousands of summer camps all over the country. You can find out about them by checking with:
- School placement office
- Friends who have been to camp
- Yellow Pages
- Camp ads in newspapers and magazines
- Library
- Camp associations (listed in Yellow Pages); the largest is the American Camping Association, in Martinsville, Indiana. (See appendix A.)

HOW TO APPLY

Decide on four or five camps that interest you, and write a letter to the director of each, requesting an application form. Most of the application forms ask for a lot of details on your background and experience. But your letter should include these facts:
- Your age
- Schooling completed
- Camping experience, either as a camper or counselor
- Any jobs held
- Skills

When you receive the form, fill it out and return it promptly. If the director is interested in hiring you, you may be asked to go for an interview.

THE INTERVIEW—
WHAT TO EXPECT

A neat appearance will make a good first impression. Blue jeans are definitely out of place here. You should arrive on time, and you should know what to expect.

The camp director is looking for a person with a pleasant personality who likes children and who can be trusted with them. Some of the questions he or she might ask you are:

- Why do you want to work in a camp?
- Why did you pick this camp?
- What do you feel you can do best for the campers?
- What did you enjoy best at your last camp?
- What did you like least?

There should also be some questions in your mind, such as:

- What would my exact responsibilities be?
- To whom would I report?
- How many children would I be in charge of?
- What age group?
- How many counselors do you have in relation to campers?
- Does the camp follow the standards set forth for accreditation by the American Camping Association? (See appendix A.)
- What are the exact dates the camp opens and closes?
- When would I be expected to report?

You should also ask about salary, laundry, medical facilities, and time off.

Remember, the questions you ask let the director know that you are thinking intelligently about the job and its responsibilities.

If you are offered a job, think it over carefully before you accept, and see if you have any more questions. If you decide it's for you, send back the signed contract promptly.

HOW TO PREPARE

Your summer as a counselor will be more fun for you and the campers if you do some preparing in the winter and spring. For instance:

- Brush up on your flute, macrame, swimming, or whatever your skill is.

- Find out if your local high school or city recreation department offers a campcraft course for counselors.

- Do some reading. Check your library for books on camping and counseling. Or write to the American Camping Association for a list of books and pamphlets.

- Consider taking a lifesaving course or a first-aid course. Certification in either of these areas, especially lifesaving, can be a big help in getting you a job at camp. The American Red Cross sponsors a number of courses via schools, YMCAs, YWCAs, and Red Cross chapters across the country. Basic Rescue and Water Safety, for example, is open to those eleven and older. It lasts for ten classes of a minimum of one hour each. Advanced Lifesaving is open to those fifteen and older. (See appendix B for more information on the American Red Cross.)

Camp directors like counselors who are skilled in one or more areas, but they also like counselors to be well-rounded, so they can help the specialists and pitch in when someone gets sick or has a day off.

The projects described in this book were selected in order to send you off to camp with "tricks up your sleeve" for amusing and instructing your young charges, for assisting the specialty counselors, and for keeping the kids happy when it rains.

So have a great summer as a SUPER camp counselor!

Arts and Crafts: Creative and Fun

All kids love to make things. Arts and crafts in a sunny outdoor setting can be a delightful and creative experience for your campers.

WHERE TO GET MATERIALS

Camp workshops are usually well-stocked with basic craft materials such as construction paper, colored tissue and cellophane paper, cardboard, shellac, and so on. But camp craft activities should include as much material gathered from the outdoors as possible. For example:

Acorns	Shells	Moss
Pine cones	Seeds	Ferns
Driftwood	Nuts	Leaves
Pebbles	Feathers	Flowers

Since there's so much you can do with pressed leaves and flowers, it's a good idea to build a flower and leaf press at the beginning of the summer. The campers can add flowers and leaves they collect on hikes, and you'll have a continuous supply for crafts.

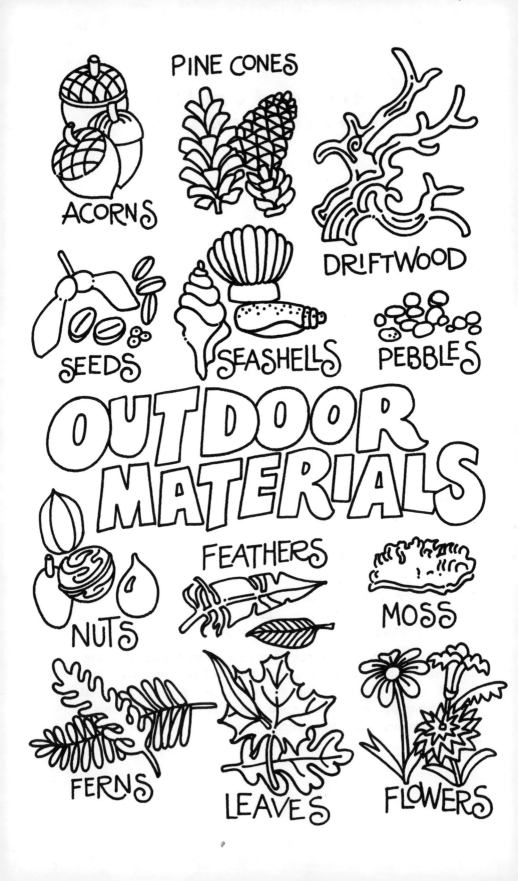

A LEAF PRESS

You need

- Two wooden boards of about 12 by 18 inches (30.4 by 45.7 cm). These will be the covers of the press.
- Sheets of blotting paper cut to the same size as the boards. Begin with about two dozen.
- Sheets of corrugated paper the same size as the blotters and boards. You need half as many as the blotters.
- Two ropes or straps long enough to go around the stack of boards, blotting paper, and corrugated paper.

Directions

1. Place leaves, blossoms or ferns between two sheets of blotting paper.
2. Stack the sets of blotting paper on top of each other, separating each set with one sheet of corrugated paper.
3. Place a wooden board underneath and on top of the stack of blotters.
4. Wrap the straps securely around the package.
5. Place a heavy weight on top.
6. After a few days, open the press and your leaves will be dried and flat, and ready for use in a craft project. (If the weather is very damp, you may need to change the blotting paper every day or two until the plants are dry.)

And if you prefer, there is another, simpler way to dry plants:

1. Lay the leaves between two layers of facial tissue.
2. Cover with a thick layer of newspapers.
3. Weigh down with a few heavy books for twenty-four hours.
4. If you like, change the tissue and press for another twenty-four hours.

Another wonderful source of craft materials is the camp kitchen. Make friends with the kitchen staffers and ask them to save items such as the following:

Egg cartons
Tin cans
Paper bags
Paper towel tubes
Used wooden matches

Corks
Bottle tops
Drinking straws
Ice cream sticks

CRAFT GUIDELINES

For a minimum of fuss, and successful results, keep these guidelines in mind:

1. Always allot enough time to finish a project. It's no fun to start something and not be able to finish it.
2. Be sure the project is simple enough for your age group and that you have all the necessary materials. To make sure, complete a sample ahead of time.
3. Give each child enough materials to work with. This means you must plan quantities needed carefully.
4. Keep only the materials you need for the project on the worktable or in the work area. There's no point in confusing things.
5. Have plenty of rags and paper towels on hand to clean up during and after the project.
6. Get things rolling by doing a short demonstration of the project. But don't actually finish it, or the group will try to copy yours and won't make any decisions for themselves. Crafts should be an exploration, not an exercise in copying.
7. If you're working with younger children, you should cut out the basic materials in advance, to save time and possible injury from scissors.

Here are a few projects campers are sure to enjoy.

"JIGSAW" MURAL

The whole group works on this together, and the result can be used to decorate the cabin or recreation room walls. If

FROM THE KITCHEN

TIN CANS

EGG CARTONS

USED WOODEN MATCHES

PAPER TOWEL TUBES

CORKS

BOTTLE CAPS

ICE CREAM STICKS

PAPER BAGS

DRINKING STRAWS

there are more than seven or eight campers in your group, divide them into smaller groups, each working on its own mural.

You need
- One piece of brown wrapping paper for each mural. The size isn't important as long as the children can work on it together. Twelve feet (3.6 m) long is a good size, but it can be smaller.
- Crayons or pastels

Directions
1. Assign each group a theme such as "A Day at Camp," "Life in the Big City," "The Forest," or "Transportation."
2. Ask them to take black chalk or crayons and draw outlines of pictures relating to the theme.
3. When they're finished, you turn the drawing over and, with pencil or crayon, divide it into *numbered* segments several inches in size, something like big jigsaw puzzle pieces.
4. Cut out these segments, but *before you cut,* make a small drawing on another piece of paper showing the locations of the segments and their numbers, to help you paste it back together again.
5. Put the cut-out segments in a box and ask the children to pick them out one by one and color in the outlines they drew. Tell them to use lots of different colors and to cover every inch of brown paper.
6. When the coloring is finished, put the mural back together with tape, following the numbers on the backs of the pieces and looking at the map you made in step 4. The result will be a lovely colorful piece of art that the children worked on together.

THREE-DIMENSIONAL PAINTING

You need
- Pieces of cardboard, about 8½ by 10 or 11 inches (21.6 by 25.4 or 27.9 cm), one for each child

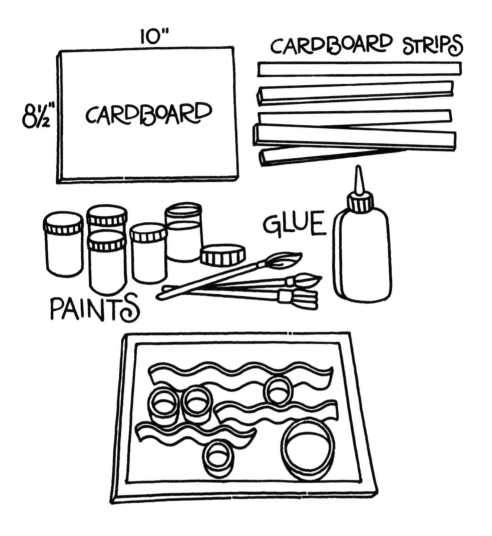

- Strips of the same cardboard, cut about ¼ inch (.6 cm) wide
- Paints
- Glue

Directions
1. Form the strips into curves, wavy lines, triangles, or any shape.
2. Brush one cut edge of the strips with paste and stick them on the cardboard, for a 3-D effect. It will look best

if each shape is repeated three or more times. Cover the cardboard with these shapes.

3. When the glue is dry, paint the whole picture, using only one color or many colors.

The finished picture can be hung on the wall, or taken home as a souvenir.

BOOKMARK

Pretty and useful, bookmarks make thoughtful presents. The campers can make a bunch of them in different colors, using some of the leaves and flowers from the press.

You need
- Heavy cardboard or construction paper cut in different shapes such as rectangles, circles, triangles, or squares, large enough to be used as bookmarks
- Dried leaves, flowers or small ferns
- Clear, self-adhesive plastic such as Contact, cut the same shapes as the paper. You need two pieces of this for every bookmark.
- Paint (optional)

Directions
1. Glue the pressed leaves or flowers in a pretty design on a piece of construction paper or cardboard. If you like, you can also paint or draw a border around the edge.
2. Peel off the backings from the clear plastic and attach one piece to the front of the bookmark and one to the back, to protect and stiffen it.

Variation: Instead of using pressed flowers, the campers could just paint scenes or geometric designs on the bookmarks and finish, as in step 2.

SAND ART

"Paintings" made of sand are attractive reminders of a summer spent by the sea or a lake.

You need

- A container of sand (strained ahead of time) for every child
- A piece of cardboard for every child. The size depends on how large a picture you want to make. Eight by 10 or 11 inches (20.3 by 25.4 or 27.9 cm) is a good size to start with. (You could also use posterboard or very smooth wood.)
- White glue
- Water to mix with the glue and a container
- Brush
- Pencil

Directions

1. Lightly draw a simple picture or design with the pencil on cardboard.
2. Brush the glue, mixed with a little water, on one section of the cardboard at a time.
3. Sprinkle the glued portion with sand, shaking off excess sand as you work.
4. Let dry overnight.

Variation: Paint the areas not covered by sand. Suggested themes for sand pictures include fish, crab, bird, starfish, simple landscapes, a sunset.

If you can get sand in different shades, you'll have an even more effective picture. You can even dye sand different colors by mixing it with berry juices, food coloring, or powdered tempera. Let it dry in the sun before using it.

PINE CONE MOBILES

Mobiles are popular craft projects, and pine cone mobiles are quick and easy to make. Even young children can make them. The mobiles can be used to decorate cabin windows, walls, and ceilings.

You need

- Pine cones. You and your group can gather these

ahead of time, perhaps on a nature walk. Choose the smaller ones ranging in size from a peanut to a walnut. Anything larger will be too heavy for this mobile.

- Heavy construction paper in various colors cut in strips 6 inches (15.2 cm) long and ¾ inches (1.9 cm) wide (longer to make a larger mobile).
- Thread
- Paste or tape

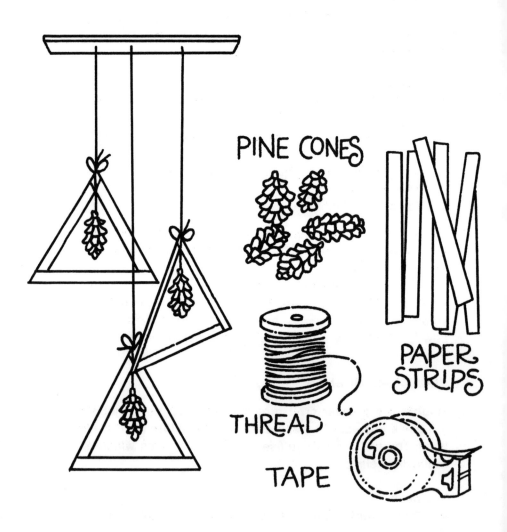

PINE CONES

PAPER STRIPS

THREAD

TAPE

Directions
1. On a flat surface, arrange three strips to form a triangle. Tape or paste ends together; trim corners.
2. Tie a piece of thread (1½ to 2 inches long) (3.8 to 5.1 cm) around the top or bottom of a pine cone and tape the thread to one corner of the triangle, so the pine cone dangles in the center.
3. Tape more thread to the top of the mobile, and make a loop to hang it from a nail in the ceiling, wall, or window frame.

Now you have a basic triangle mobile. You can add more triangles to make a larger mobile. Or have the campers in your group tape their mobiles together to make one huge one.

If your camp is near the seashore, you can use small shells instead of pine cones, or a combination of both.

EGG CARTON BOX

When finished, this box can be used to display rock or shell collections, or store jewelry and other treasures.

You need
- Empty egg cartons, one for each child. Your pals in the camp kitchen should be able to supply you with these.
- Paint and brushes
- All sorts of decorations from nature sources or otherwise —anything that can be glued onto the carton
- Glue

Directions
1. Paint the carton, inside and out. You might want to use different colors on the outside, and perhaps paint the inside of each egg-holder a different color.
2. Glue on the trimmings. Let the kids use their imaginations. Here are some suggestions:

Cover the top entirely with shells, small pine cones, colorful pebbles, or seeds.

Paste just one long, graceful leaf or flower on the lid.

Glue on yarn in floral or geometric shapes.

MORE CRAFT IDEAS

- Make pipe-cleaner people, using nuts or pine cones for heads.
- Make *papier-mâché* puppet heads, using paper towel tubing for sticks.
- Make mobiles from basket weaving materials. Shape the caning into circles; cover with colored tissue paper or cellophane paper for a stained-glass effect.
- Using colored modeling clay, ask the children to make their favorite shoe. For example, a sneaker, running shoe, high-heeled shoe.
- Read a story or poem to the children and have them make a scene from it, using whatever materials they want. Give them a choice of, say, clay, *papier-mâché,* found objects, paint, or crayons.
- Make holiday wreaths, using Styrofoam circles and large pine cones.
- Create a mosaic picture using pebbles gathered from the beach or lake front.
- Make paperweights using rocks with pieces of felt glued on. Paint funny faces on the rocks.

Nature:
Leaves, Rocks, and Stars

Being out of doors and learning about nature is one of the real pleasures of camp life.

Counselors don't have to be trained naturalists to help their young charges discover nature. In fact, it can be a joint learning experience.

RAMBLE THROUGH NATURE

A slow walk through the woods is probably the best all-around nature activity. Keep these tips in mind for successful nature rambles:

- Wear long pants and a shirt with long sleeves to protect against insect bites, scratches, and sunburn. Shorts aren't a good idea on a hike.
- Wear sturdy shoes or sneakers, and socks. Bare feet don't hike well.
- Bring a pocket magnifying glass.
- Don't forget containers to bring back good "finds" such as leaves or flowers to be pressed, unusual pebbles, seeds, and insects.
- Carry a pedometer to measure your distance.

- If you bring a knife, keep it in a sheath when you're not using it.
- Use a compass and teach your charges how to use it.
- Bring water or fruit juices if you're going on a long walk.
- If you have a large group, ask another counselor to come with you, to make sure no one gets lost.
- Appoint a responsible camper to be at the end of the line, to make sure no one gets left behind. With younger children, use the "buddy system" to form pairs.
- Stop often to look, listen, smell, touch.

To get the most out of a nature ramble, teach the campers to use their senses. For instance:

Look!
Pick out all the different colors of nature. How many shades of green can you see? Does anyone see something red? Can you find a purple flower? Look for trees in funny shapes. Watch for tiny animals and insects. What are they doing? Identify the flowers and berries you see along the way.

Listen!
How many different sounds do you hear? Birds chattering? Water splashing or dripping? An animal rustling in the woods? Cars on a highway? Complete silence?

Smell!
Can you smell flowers? Pine trees? Herbs? Cut grass? Wood burning? Salty ocean air? A skunk?

Touch!
What does an acorn feel like? Is the earth moist or dry? Rub your finger on the edge of a leaf. Compare how the barks of different trees feel.

MAKE AN INSECT FARM

The care and feeding of insects can be fascinating, as well as educational. To make a home for insects, you need:

- A container such as a clear plastic box or a jar

- Soil and a grassy sod to put in the bottom of the container, along with a twig or small branch
- Screening or mosquito netting to tie over the top of the "cage"

Directions
1. Keep different kinds of insects in different cages.
2. Feed your insects every day. Grasshoppers will eat the grass growing in the cage. Crickets like tiny pieces of bread soaked in water, and bits of lettuce. And caterpillars like grass or clover.
3. Water the grass in the cage to keep it fresh and growing.
4. Don't leave uneaten food in the cage. Keep the cage clean.
5. At the end of the camp session, return the insects to their natural home.

Read about the habits of these insects in an insect book and discuss them with the campers.

PRESERVE ANIMAL TRACKS

Animal tracks preserved in plaster make unique camp souvenirs.

You need
- A small bag of plaster of paris (Buy it at a hardware or drug store.)
- Strips of cardboard
- Small can of talcum powder
- Tin can for mixing the plaster
- Water

Directions
1. Look for interesting animal tracks on your nature ramble.
2. Sprinkle the track with talcum powder, to keep the plaster cast clean.
3. Surround the track with a strip of the cardboard. Push it into the ground a little to hold it in place.

4. Mix some water with plaster of paris in the tin can, until the plaster is as thick as heavy cream or pancake batter. Add a tiny pinch of salt to make it set faster.
5. Pour the plaster of paris over the track, inside the cardboard collar. Let it set.
6. When dry, lift the cast and remove the cardboard.

If you like, you can paint the finished cast. If you want to make a hanging plaque, insert a paper clip in the plaster before it hardens.

Try to find tracks left by animals walking, running, and standing still. Make casts and compare the differences.

Variation: You can also make plaster casts of leaves, flowers, and ferns. Here's how:

1. Pour the plaster of paris into a mold.
2. Dampen the leaf or flower with a little water and place it on the plaster.
3. Go over it with a paintbrush to make sure the entire surface is in contact with the plaster.
4. Remove the leaf when the plaster is half dry.
5. Let the plaster dry completely.

SCAVENGER HUNT

Divide your group into teams or pairs. Give each team a list of objects from nature they must find within a certain amount of time. Here's part of a sample list:

Maple leaf
Mushroom
Small red pebble
Bird feather
One pine cone the size of an egg
One pine cone as small as a thimble
Five pine needles in a cluster
One dandelion
Small rock
Piece of moss

MAPLE
LEAF

MUSHROOM

SMALL RED PEBBLE

BIRD
FEATHER

PINE CONE
(SIZE OF EGG)

PINE CONE
(SMALL AS THIMBLE)

FIVE PINE NEEDLES

ONE
DANDELION

SMALL ROCK

PIECE OF
MOSS

Variation: Ask for:
  Something small
  Something large
  Something light
  Something heavy
  Something that smells good
  Something that smells bad
  Something pretty
  Something ugly
  Something wet
  Something dry
and so on. Obviously, your lists will be based on the wildlife around your camp.

The first team or pair to complete the list wins.

"POISONOUS" FLASH CARDS

1. Paste pictures of poisonous and nonpoisonous plants, berries, and snakes in your region on individual cards.
2. Flash them one at a time. The person who identifies the most wins the first half of the game.
3. Flash them again. The person who identifies the highest number of poisonous and nonpoisonous species wins the second half of the game.

Variation: The person or team that both correctly identifies the most items, and knows whether they are poisonous or not wins. This game is a good way to teach the campers about dangers in the area.

HIKING-LIST CONTEST

On one of your hikes, take along a list of about twenty items your group might see along the way. Assign points to each item. The first camper to see an item and report it to you scores. Whoever gets the highest score of the day is the winner and resident "nature expert."

Here's a sample list:

Frog—5 points
Chipmunk—10 points
Squirrel tracks—15 points
Butterfly—10 points
Bird's nest—10 points (Don't disturb!)

LEAF RACE

1. Divide group into teams or pairs.
2. Allow them ten minutes to gather one leaf from as many different trees as they can.
3. When they bring the leaves back, they must correctly identify them.
4. The team with the most correctly identified leaves wins.

NAME THE STARS

You need
- A large can with an electric bulb inserted into it
- Pieces of cardboard large enough to cover the opening of the can

Directions
1. Punch holes in the cardboard to represent constellations.
2. Hold the pieces over the light so the constellations flash on the wall.
3. Campers try to identify the star formations. Each correct guess earns 1 point.

MAKE A FISH PRINT

You need
- One recently caught fish, not yet skinned or cleaned
- Oil paint or watercolor paint
- Artist's paper

Directions
1. Roll the fish in the paint.

2. Carefully roll it on the paper. Every scale and fin should show up.

OTHER NATURE IDEAS

- Build a bird house. Watch the birds that inhabit it and keep a diary of their activities.
- Make a quill pen from a large bird feather. Cut the end of the quill on the slant.
- Plant a wild-flower garden.
- Make a cabin nature scrapbook. Include pressed leaves, drawings of flowers and insects, notes on birds in the area, the life story of a butterfly, and so on.
- Save seeds from watermelons and cantaloupes for use in crafts.
- Make candleholders from knotholes in pieces of wood.
- Find out what plants and berries in your area are edible, and have a "back to nature" picnic.
- Use a chunk of moss as a paintbrush. Pin down a leaf on paper and spatter paint around it with your mossy paintbrush.
- Start a cabin rock collection. Use the egg carton containers described in the chapter on "Arts and Crafts," pages 17 and 18.
- Make "rock folk." Select different sizes of rocks. Use some as heads, bodies, hands, feet. Paint faces and clothes on them.

Splish-Splash:
Water Games and Races

Not all water activities involve swimming. Children can run, hop, or jump in shallow water. Playing games is the best way to get them used to water, and to build up their confidence for learning to swim. Remember, just as in playing games on dry land, you should limit the play area in the water.

Games for beginners

Balloons can add color and fun to water activities. Here's one of many balloon games:

BALLOON BINGO

You need
- Uninflated balloons on which numbers have been written (one number—0 to 9—per balloon)

Directions
1. Divide the group into two teams with home bases on opposite sides of the pool or swimming area.
2. Give each team member a balloon and tell them to scatter all over the swimming area.

3. Call out a number, for instance, 589; 2000; 48,235. Everyone swims, dog-paddles, or runs to his or her side of the swimming area, gets out, and blows up the balloon. Those with the numbers called out must line up in proper order. For example, if you call out "589," those with balloons numbered 5, 8, and 9 must stand next to each other in that order. If there are duplicate numbers, they form lines. In other words, the 5s line up next to the 8s and the 9s line up next to them. Those without the numbers called jump back into the water. The first team to form the number correctly and have its other members back in the water wins.

Variation: Use letters instead of numbers.

PENNY DIVE

This works best in a pool, where you can see the bottom clearly. Toss a handful of pennies into the pool. When you blow a whistle, the kids jump in and gather as many as they can within a certain amount of time. They score one point for each penny.

You can also use buttons or pebbles instead of pennies.

Or you can use corks which, of course, will float instead of sink. Paint the corks different colors and assign them different number values.

Land games such as "follow the leader" and "tug-of-war" can also be played in the pool or lake. Here's a watery version of an old favorite:

SIMON SAYS

This is a useful game to help beginners practice different swimming strokes.

Just as in the land game, the swimmers do what "Simon says." For example, "Simon says, float"; "Simon says, do the breast stroke"; "Simon says, tread water."

If you omit the words "Simon says" when you give the command, the swimmers must ignore it. They get one point for each mistake. The winner is the one with the least number of points.

WATER TAG

Games of tag are as popular in the water as they are on dry land. In most cases you don't need equipment. It can be as simple as having one person, "it," trying to tag the others, all "running" as fast as they can in shallow water. Here are a few variations:

PARTNER TAG

1. Pair your group off into twos. Each pair must hold hands.
2. One pair is "it." They try to tag other pairs.
3. If a pair breaks hands to avoid "it," they automatically become "it."

BALL TAG

"It" tries to tag the others by throwing a soft foam ball or an inflated ball. Whoever is hit becomes "it."

TEAM TAG

1. Divide the group into two teams, with each team member having a letter or number (A, B, C or 1, 2, 3, and so on).
2. The two teams face each other in the water.
3. You, as the leader, throw a ball into the water, between the two teams, and call out a letter (or number); for example, "C."
4. The C swimmers from each team swim toward the ball.
5. The first to reach it takes it and tries to swim back to his or her team, with the swimmer from the other team following.

6. If the swimmer with the ball reaches home, that team scores a point. But if he or she is tagged by the other swimmer, the other team scores.
The team that wins the highest number of points wins.

PING-PONG FLOAT

You need
- A Ping-Pong ball and plastic drinking straw for each swimmer

Directions
1. Line up the campers in waist-high water.
2. When you whistle, they put the straws in their mouths and each tries to blow a Ping-Pong ball across the water.
3. The first one to reach the other side of the swimming area is the winner.

PIGGYBACK RACE

1. Match up partners of equal weight and have one climb on the shoulders of the other, piggyback style.
2. Tell each pair to walk from one side of the pool to the other.
3. They switch positions at the other side for the trip back home. The first pair to return to the starting side wins.

WATER CAROUSEL

This one combines fun 'n' games with floating practice. There are no winners or losers.

1. One person is "it."
2. The other swimmers form a circle of pairs with an A and B in each pair.
3. They start moving around in the circle, just like a carousel, gradually getting faster.
4. At one point the leader says, "All the A's float." The A's

float on their backs while their partners pull them. Then the leader decides that "B's float," and so on.

Tip: Experienced leaders know to end activities and games *before* campers get tired. End each when the fun is at its peak so the children will want to do it again later.

Games for inter-mediate swimmers

WATER BALL

You need
- One ball (soft)

Directions
1. The children form a circle in shallow water, with you, the leader, in the center, holding the ball.
2. When you call out a child's name, he or she swims toward you to get the ball, while the others swim away from you.
3. When the child gets the ball, he or she calls out "Stop." The other swimmers must stop, and the child with the ball tries to hit one of the others with it. Anyone who is hit has a point scored against him or her. Those with three points leave the game.

HANDBALL IN THE WATER

You need
- Two balls (large)

Directions
1. Divide the group into two teams; each team has a separate goal.
2. Each team must push its ball, using hands or feet, toward its own goal.
3. The team that scores the most goals wins.

WATER BATTLE

You need
- Two flags, or other objects to use as flags

Directions
1. Two teams line up at opposite sides of the pool or swimming area.
2. They move toward each other and try to capture the other team's flag and bring it back to their own side.
3. A point is scored every time the opposing team's flag is captured and brought "home."

APPLE RELAY RACE

You need
- Apples

Directions
1. Float the apples in the center of the pool or swimming area.
2. Divide the group into two teams and line them up along the edge of the swimming area.
3. When you give a signal, one team member from each group dives for an apple, grabs it and swims back to the starting point.
4. When he or she reaches home, another team member dives in and tries to get an apple.
5. The team with the most apples wins.

HAT RACE

You need
- One hat for each swimmer

Directions
1. Line up the swimmers in the water.

2. When you give the signal, they submerge, losing their hats.
3. They surface immediately and try to get their hats back on their head without using their hands, and swim to the edge of the pool, or other marker.

WATER WHEELBARROW RACE

1. Divide the group into pairs.
2. One partner floats on the water while the other holds his or her ankles.
3. When you give the signal, the "wheelbarrows" race to the other side of the swimming area, pushing and paddling. ("Wheelbarrows" may use their arms to keep themselves above water.)
4. The first pair to reach the other side wins.

All the Camp's a Stage: Drama and Music

Kids love to "ham it up" when it comes to acting and singing. After a few shy moments, you'll have an enthusiastic group of performers, whether it's for their own enjoyment, or for the audience of an "all campers" show.

DRAMATIC ACTIVITIES

The most important thing children get from drama is self-expression—a chance to say or act what they feel. Simple mimes and improvisations are good for this, and easy to do. Keep these drama guidelines in mind:

- Make the project fun, so the children don't feel self-conscious.
- Get everyone involved. But don't make a child participate who really doesn't want to. Just say, "OK, you be the audience." Learning to be a good audience is important, too. And if you're putting on a real play, the kids who don't want to perform can take care of props, costumes, programs, and so on.
- Have the campers perform drama projects in groups rather than one by one.

- Have a specific project in mind, but leave room for the kids' imaginations to take over.
- Keep things simple. In camp performances, there's no need for elaborate costumes or scenery. You can use pieces of campers' and counselors' clothing, make masks from paper bags, use crepe paper and camp furniture for scenery.

A few drama projects

MAKE A COMMERCIAL

1. Divide the group into smaller groups of about six campers.
2. Tell them to make up a TV commercial advertising anything they want. If they seem to have trouble finding an idea, give them suggestions, such as "a new mouthwash," "a compact car," "potato chips," "a toy."
3. Appoint a group leader to make sure everyone cooperates.
4. Give them about ten minutes to plan their commercials. When ten minutes are up, ask if they need more time.
5. When everyone is ready, have the groups perform their commercials in turn.

This is a good project for campers over six years old. The seven- and eight-year-olds may do better working in pairs or threes, rather than in larger groups.

THE "FEELING" GLASSES, OR "MAGIC GLASSES"

This project helps kids get to know different feelings.

1. Everyone wears a pair of glasses, real or imaginary.
2. They "take them off" and walk around.
3. You say, "OK, when you put your glasses on again,

everything will look happy." The idea is for the children to imagine they're looking at happy things, and to express happy feelings. Other emotions can be used—for example, fear, triumph, surprise.

Variation: In a craft session, make "magic glasses" for use in this game. Use cardboard and wire. Paint the glasses and decorate them with sequins and braid so they look glittery and gaudy.

GROUP IMPROVISATION

Ask the group to decide upon:

- An opening line of a scene
- A closing line
- The number of characters in a scene
- A season
- A location where the scene will take place

Then they act out the scene, improvising as they go along. This works well with ages seven and up. For younger children, just ask them to supply opening and closing lines. You help them with the rest.

Variation: Ask the group to act out a specific situation, for example, "stuck in an elevator." Before they start, ask them to decide on a few details: time of day, who they are, what kind of building they are in, season, where have they come from, where are they going.

Results of this improvisation can be hilarious.

FOLLOW THE LEADER

Set up certain spaces in the play area where only certain activities can take place. For instance: in one spot "You have to move fast"; in another part "You have to move slowly"; in another area "Gravity doesn't exist"; and in another section "You can't use your feet to move around."

Everyone gets in line and follows the leader, you, through this incredible maze.

NURSERY RHYME CHARADES

Think up a collection of charades based on nursery rhymes that groups of two or more children can act out, and the others have to guess. Write them on pieces of paper and put them in a box.

1. Ask each group to pick one out of the box.
2. Allow them about ten minutes to plan their charade.
3. Make sure they know that no talking is allowed during the charade.

Besides using nursery rhymes, you can pick out certain events that take place in fairy tales. For example:

- Cinderella losing her slipper
- Goldilocks meeting the three bears
- Jack climbing the beanstalk

For older campers, think up more complicated situations, such as:

- Two people chasing a butterfly through quicksand
- Passengers on a plane trying to land on an icy runway
- Swimming in a pool of molasses

MUSICAL ACTIVITIES

Singing around the campfire is a popular camp activity. The more songs you know, the more fun it is. So don't go off to camp without one or two good songbooks. And no doubt the camp library will have a selection.

When picking songs for your group, keep these suggestions in mind:

- Look for humorous songs.
- Pick songs with a strong rhythm.
- Use songs the campers know before starting new ones.
- Encourage the singers to clap, sway, and tap their feet as they sing.
- Look for songs with repeating choruses.
- Sing songs from other countries.

Here's an unusual suggestion for getting everybody into the "sing." A group leader or counselor says, "OK, we'll sing songs with colors in them." The group is divided into smaller groups, and the group that keeps coming up with the most songs is the winner. (Sample songs: "Scarlet Ribbons"; "Yellow Submarine"; "I Dream of Jeannie with the Light Brown Hair.")

Variation: Songs with boys' names; girls' names; names of animals; flowers; and so on.

ORGANIZE A CAMPERS' PERCUSSION BAND

Make your own musical instruments. This could be a good craft activity also. Here are some ideas:

Drums: Use any round container such as an oatmeal box, with one end open. Stretch any heavy material such as canvas or plastic across the opening, and attach with thumbtacks or rubber bands. Make drumsticks from wooden sticks. You can also attach an empty thread spool to a stick.

Triangles: Any large piece of metal can be used as a triangle. Use a heavy nail to beat it with.

Tambourines: A tinfoil pie plate, with bells or bottle caps attached.

Maracas, or rattles: Fill a cardboard box, wooden box, or tin can with seeds, pebbles, or nuts. Seal the open end and attach a handle. Or make holes in both ends and insert a handle through the rattle.

Different contents of the maracas will give different sounds.

Rhythm sticks: Two straight sticks about a foot (.3 m) long. Sand until smooth. Paint or shellac.

The kids are bound to have their own ideas, too, on how to make instruments. When they're done, your group can give a concert or participate in the camp talent night.

Games
Campers Play

There's nothing like playing a few fast, active games for breaking the ice and helping campers get to know one another.

Most of the games in this section can be played by boys and girls of all ages. But since a fourteen-year-old will be more skillful than an eight-year-old, you should not mix the ages too much.

There are all kinds of games—quiet games, noisy games, active games, circle games, line games, games where everyone is standing, games where everyone sits. But games are more fun when winning and losing are not as important as everyone having a good time.

One important thing to remember is, whether you play outdoors or indoors, set up boundaries inside which the game must be played, or things might get out of control. Outside, use fences, picnic tables, or sticks as markers. Inside, use pieces of furniture or floor markings.

Also, try to have something else going on nearby, so that as players are eliminated from one game, they don't have to sit on the sidelines, waiting for it to end.

Don't be afraid to let the children use their imaginations and make up their own games or add variations to the games you play with them. Try out their suggestions.

BARNYARD

This is suitable for a group of about twelve to twenty campers.

Directions

1. Whisper to each child the name of a farm animal. Use only three or four different animals, depending on the size of the group, so that, for example, several of them will be sheep; others will represent horses, chickens, ducks, and so on.
2. Direct the whole group to close their eyes and move around on hands and knees, making the sound of whatever animal each one is. For example, the "cows" will moo; the "pigs" will oink; the "ducks" will quack; and so on.
3. The object of the game is for all the "animals" to gather in their own groups by listening to the noises they are making. The first group to gather is the winning group.

The game should keep going until all the groups have "found" each other.

With older children, you might want to make one camper the only "dog," for example. When all the groups assemble, only the "dog" is still looking for a group. Be sure you pick a good sport for this one, and, afterwards, give this "animal" a special prize such as a "dog biscuit" (cookie or cupcake).

"MIRROR, MIRROR"

This game takes a bit of concentration, so it's better for older children.

Directions
1. Divide your group into pairs and line them up facing each other. Line A is "reality"; line B is "mirror."
2. The leader counts aloud slowly—1, 2, 3, etc. At each count, the children in line A make a gesture, such as pull an ear, wink, turn their heads, and so on. The "mirrors" must reflect the action, just like a real mirror. For example, if a participant winks the left eye, the "mirror" facing him or her must wink the right eye.

Start this game off simply, using only head movements, for example. Then allow them to use arm and leg movements. There's no real winner. Only a lot of laughs and plenty of coordination practice.

Tag games

Tag is one of the oldest games there is, and there are many variations. Here are just a few:

FREEZE TAG

This is good for any group of seven or more children. One camper is "it." "It" runs around among the others, trying to "tag" them. As each child is tagged, he or she must "freeze" and hold that position for the rest of the game. The game ends when everyone is "freezing." If you like, you can give a prize for the funniest "freeze."

This game works best with older children (over ten). They can stay in one position longer than younger ones who do better with a lot of movement.

SNAKE IN THE GRASS

The child who is "it" is the snake in the grass and lies on his or her stomach on the ground. The other children dare to run as close to the snake as possible without being tagged by the snake's arms or legs which are waving around.

Each child who is tagged becomes a snake, too. The more snakes there are, the more difficult it gets for the children running around to avoid being tagged. The game ends when everyone is a snake.

HOPPING TAG

Directions
1. Divide the group into two teams and line them up against two facing walls. In the outdoors, mark off imaginary walls.
2. Select one child to be "it."
3. "It" must command everyone to "hop." At the command, the two lines of children must hop toward each other, to the other wall. "It" must also hop, as he or she tries to tag the others. The child who is tagged becomes "it" and must give a different command. Commands could include run, skip, slide, crawl, or walk pigeon-toed.

Again, there's no real winner in this game. It's played just for fun.

Relay races

Relay races are good for the campers because they teach them to work as a team, rather than to just try to win for themselves. These two relay races combine fun with team spirit:

PONY AND RIDER

Directions
1. Divide the children into pairs of "ponies" and "riders."

The pony stands with arms extended to the back. The rider stands behind the pony and holds its hands.

2. When the race begins, they all gallop to a certain spot, where they turn around and switch positions. In other words, the riders become the ponies.
3. The first team to complete a certain number of runs, switching positions, is the winning pair.

BEANBAG BOUNCE

Directions
1. Line up two teams of equal numbers at the starting line.
2. Mark a goal about 20 feet (6.1 m) away.
3. When you give the signal, player number one from each team kicks the beanbag over the goal line, runs and picks it up, and runs back to the starting line. The first one back scores a point for his or her team.
4. You give the signal again, and the second player on each team kicks, runs, and returns.
5. The game is over when each player has had one turn. The team with the most points wins.

Tip: Don't overexplain a new activity. Your campers will lose their enthusiasm with windy introductions. Start the game as soon as possible, adding rules along the way.

A Rainy Day at Camp

Believe it or not, a wet day at summer camp is not a disaster. It can actually mean a welcome change of pace, such as more rest for everyone, and some quiet times around a fireplace.

Some activities such as crafts, music and drama, and games can still go on. Just move them indoors. Of course, space inside may be a bit cramped, so the activities should be on the quiet side, with not too much moving around. Instead of holding a relay race, play games with everyone sitting on the floor in a circle.

This is also a good time to plan surprises and little extras, to help campers forget the dreary weather, especially if it's been raining for a few days. For instance:

- A costume party
- A talent show
- Special meals (such as a candlelight dinner)

Or, celebrate Halloween a little early, complete with funny get-ups and trick-or-treating. Or you could celebrate Thanksgiving with a turkey dinner, or Christmas with a tree and homemade presents.

Save some projects just for a rainy day.

GO OUTDOORS IN THE RAIN

Wet weather need not cancel that hike or swim you had planned, as long as there isn't a thunderstorm. In fact, the rain can add novelty to outdoor activities.

Swimming in the rain. Play lots of water games and keep the kids moving and active. Dry off quickly, put on warm clothes, and have a hot drink.

Hiking. First make sure everyone is dressed for the rain. Plan a short hike. Point out to the campers how different things look when it's raining. Tree trunks are shiny and dark. There are different smells and sounds. Listen to the rain falling on the leaves; hear the wind blowing. What do insects do when it rains? Can you hear birds singing in the rain?

Such a hike could be the highlight of a rainy day, especially if there's hot chocolate and marshmallows to look forward to.

TELL STORIES

Storytelling is an ancient art and rainy days or evenings at camp can provide a perfect setting for ghost stories, funny stories, fairy tales, and make-it-up-yourself stories.

When you tell stories—
- Only tell ones you enjoy yourself.
- Pick stories with a lot of action.
- Use different tones of voice to emphasize certain parts of the story.
- Look at the children as you tell the story, to include them in it.
- Use occasional gestures.

Let the campers tell stories, too. They can share favorite tales, or they can tell about something they did in the last year, such as learning to ski; moving to a new house; raising a hamster.

But the best fun is when you and your group make up your own stories as you go along. There are several ways to do that. Here are two:

FILL-IN-THE-BLANK STORIES

Directions
1. Ahead of time, select a story from a book, or make one up. But leave out most of the nouns. (This could also work with verbs or adjectives.)
2. Write out nouns on slips of paper and put them into a shoe box—for example, "one-eyed toad," "old soldier," "secret garden."
3. As you tell the story, the children pass the box and each one picks out a piece of paper and reads it when you pause for a missing word. Results can really be funny.

LIST STORIES

Directions
1. List groups of items on index cards.
2. Divide your group into smaller groups.
3. Give each group a card and tell them to make up a story using the items on the card.
4. Allow them ten minutes.

Here are a few ideas of what to put on the cards:
- A black cat; a telephone pole; a spaceship; a paper bag
- A skyscraper; an elm tree; a little girl; summer camp
- A table; a painting; a magic dragon; blue jeans
- A wicked witch; a rainstorm; a lawn; a fat book

And here's an idea for a group craft activity:

MAKE A MODEL OF THE CAMP

You need
- Modeling clay
- Cardboard to make buildings

- Pine cones or twigs painted green for trees
- Mirror for lake or pool
- Pebbles or sand for beach or lakeshore
- Pieces of toothpicks and pipe cleaners to make tiny people
- Paint
- Glue

Have different groups working on different parts of the project.

And after a watermelon-eating contest, you'll be bound to have enough material to:

MAKE A SEED PUPPET

You and your group could plan a puppet show around seed puppets. Here's how to make the puppet:

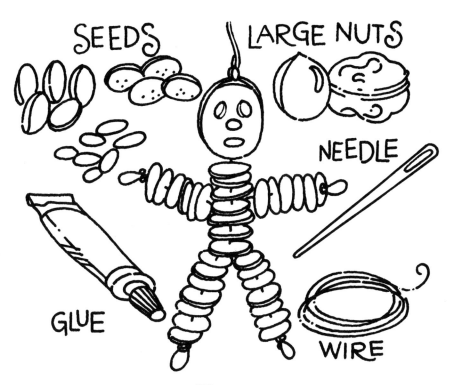

SEEDS   LARGE NUTS   NEEDLE   GLUE   WIRE

You need
- Seeds from watermelon, cantaloupe, squash, pumpkins. You can use any or all of them, and also sunflower seeds.
- Fine, flexible wire cut in lengths of 2½, 3, and 4 inches (6.4, 7.6, and 10.2 cm).
- Large nuts
- Glue
- Needle

Directions
1. Punch holes in the seeds with the needle to string them on the wire.
2. String seeds on a 3-inch (7.6-cm) piece of wire for the legs, and a 2½-inch (6.4-cm) piece for the arms. Twist the ends of the wire to hold the seeds in place. Bend the 3-inch (7.6-cm) piece in the middle to form the legs.
3. Twist a 4-inch (10.2-cm) wire to the center of the leg piece. String seeds for about 1 inch (2.5 cm), for the body.
4. Twist that wire to the center of the arm string.
5. Add seeds to the rest of that wire and loop it to form the head.
6. Glue a nut over the loop to form a face.
7. Glue on smaller seeds to form eyes, nose, and mouth.
8. Attach a string to the head for use in the puppet show.

While one group is making puppets, other campers can be writing the script for a play, and others can prepare a small theater.

Play Games Indoors

Everything from quizzes to musical chairs goes over well on damp days. The younger children are bound to enjoy this one.

BALLOON FLOAT

Directions
1. Give each child an inflated balloon.
2. Tell them to throw their balloons in the air and try to catch them before they hit the ground.
3. Whoever keeps his or her balloon in the air the longest is the winner.

You can make this game more challenging for older children by telling them they can only hit the balloon with, say, their heads or their elbows.

Here's a group game that will teach campers what cooperation is all about:

THE PEOPLE PUPPET

This works best with a large group, at least twenty campers.

1. Get them lined up in the shape of a stick figure. For example, a few campers stand in a circle to form a head. Then you need a longer line to form a body. Then arms and legs.
2. Give the figure a name; for example, Sylvester.
3. Command Sylvester to do various things. For example:

"Sylvester, move your right arm!"
"Bend to the right!"
"Scratch your head!"

The children who form the different parts of Sylvester must all move at the same time, in the direction needed to perform the activity.

MORE RAINY-DAY IDEAS

- Learn folk dancing.
- Sing songs about the rain; alternate them with songs about bright, sunshiny weather.

- Put on a camper news show.
- Hold craft workshops and a knot-tying workshop.
- Learn Morse code.
- Spend time sorting various collections of rocks, leaves, feathers.
- Write poetry about the rain.
- Make up a cabin story. The counselor starts it and each camper adds to it.
- Hold a cabin play-reading.
- Clean and redecorate the cabin. For example, use natural dyes and make new curtains. Paint murals.
- Have a bubble-blowing contest. Who can blow the biggest?
- Write letters home.
- Bring the cabin diary up to date.

A FINAL WORD

Remember, the ideas in this book are just to start you off. Once you arrive at camp, meet the kids, and get to know them, you'll find yourself making up all kinds of activities. And don't be surprised if the campers come up with good suggestions, too. They might even give you ideas you can use in following summers at camp!

Appendix A:
The American Camping Association

The American Camping Association publishes hundreds of books and pamphlets on camping. Prospective counselors may write to the ACA for their *Catalog of Selected Camping Publications.*

Also available is a pamphlet describing ACA camp standards, called *Condensed Standards for Organized Camps.* And of interest to parents is *Parents' Guide to Accredited Camps,* in four regional editions. Order blanks are available from ACA.

The American Camping Association
Bradford Woods
Martinsville, Indiana 46151

Appendix B:
The American
Red Cross

To locate lifesaving and first-aid courses in your city or community, get in touch with your local Red Cross chapter. There are thirty-one hundred chapters across the country, and many have branches.

For course descriptions and for location of chapters, write to the Director of Safety Programs at one of the following regional offices:

American Red Cross, Eastern Area
615 N. St. Asaph St.
Alexandria, VA 22314

American Red Cross, Southeastern Area
1955 Monroe Drive, NE
Atlanta, GA 30324

American Red Cross, Western Area
1870 Ogden Dr.
P.O. Box 909
Burlingame, CA 94010

American Red Cross, Midwestern Area
10195 Corporate Sq.
St. Louis, MO 63132

Bibliography

Athey, Margaret, and Hotchkiss, Gwen. *A Galaxy of Games for the Music Class.* Nyack, N.Y.: Parker Publishing Co., 1975.

Bale, R. O. *What on Earth.* Martinsville, Ind.: American Camping Association, 1969.

Gardner, John F. *A Book of Nature Activities.* Danville, Ill.: The Interstate Printers and Publishers, 1967.

Mackay, Joy. *Raindrops Keep Falling on My Tent.* Wheaton, Ill.: SP Publications, 1972.

Mitchell, Viola A.; Crawford, Ida B.; and Robberson, Julia D. *Camp Counseling.* Philadelphia: W. B. Saunders Co., 1970.

Musselman, Virginia W. *The Day Camp Program Book: An Activity Guide for Counselors.* New York: Association Press, 1963.

Nelson, Esther L. *Movement Games for Children of All Ages.* New York: Sterling Publishing Co., 1975.

Pack-O-Fun staff, eds. *Nature Crafts.* Park Ridge, Ill.: Clapper Publishing Co., a Pack-O-Fun publication, 1976.

Sholtis, M. G. *Swimnastics Is Fun.* Washington, D.C.: American Alliance for Health, Physical Education, and Recreation, 1975.

Index